PARENTING

IS A

VERB

The Art of Unlocking
Your Baby's Potential

⁂⦃⦄⁂

KIA M. HASELRIG-OPARAH

Dedication

This book is dedicated to my parents. All of these years, I was listening and learning. Buby and I have always had the best role models for parenting.

Mommy, you always made Buby and I feel like being a parent was the best job in the world! You made us a priority and I appreciate you for that. Now that we have our own babies, I totally get it. I feel the same joy for my babies! You were right! Aside from professional goals, I have always wanted a family. I always wanted to be like you and hoped I could be even half as amazing as you are.

Daddy, I have fond memories of the unique things I did with my you like learning how to use power tools, learning about the parts of a car engine, camping with my school, doing crafts like making belts with gemp, and making tents out of trash bags for my AFJROTC Survival Weekend. You set the bar high for any man who entered my life. Thank you!

Chinenye, parenting with you was Divinely Ordered. Happy we were recruited to be on the same parenting team. Left side...

To my heartbeats: Kemery and Jeremy, you make my heart smile and bring me joy every day. Our love is in our hearts and extends beyond the beats. We will always be connected by our hearts and our dreams. May you continue to explore the world around you and view the world with an open heart and with joy in your spirit.

Foreword

I remember it like it was yesterday. Almost 10 years ago when I met Kia Haselrig-Oparah, our children were in a language school studying Japanese, French, and English in a full immersion environment with native teachers. We were in awe of how much those little brains absorbed in such record times. It is one thing to read about it in books or theory as we did with our formative education, but to see actual proof of trilingual babies, accelerated learners, and true right brain, left brain convergence was exceptional. Wow, I thought. What a feat we had before us, to train these little ones up the way they should go and to prepare them to be citizens of the world. If they can accomplish being trilingual at 2 and 3, what else could they do? We both knew we had our work cut out for us to teach our children beyond the book, beyond the bell and even beyond borders. Every parent knows as George Santayana posits, "a child only educated at school is an uneducated child". What I didn't know at the time however, is there is an art to developing the skills that truly unlock your baby's potential.

As a trained school psychologist, mom and wife, Kia always had the best therapeutic responses to any of life's woes. By trade, she was familiar with the latest in psychoeducational assessments and had worked with children and families in many capacities. An encouraging word here and a tidbit there was always a welcomed treat to get throughout each day. What has been helpful on this journey is having parents and friends like Kia, who of like mind and similar paths let you know you're not alone and there are skills you can adapt to make your life easier. Kia Haselrig-Oparah is a true facilitator and prudent artist when it comes to the artistry of parenting.

Have you ever held your baby to put him to sleep, but he wouldn't fall asleep until you held him a certain way? The way *he* preferred it. There was an art to holding your baby. This is the same premise of this book and the art of unlocking your baby's genius. Life is full of inconsistencies and unpredictable happenings but nothing reflects the gravity of this phenomenon like the vicissitudes of parenting. You have to find what works for you and your family. As a wife, mom and entrepreneur, I felt like I was spread too thin to have enough time or energy for anyone after a long day. I had always sought ways to simplify my life and maximize time with my family; to ultimately give my family the best of me, not the rest of me. It had always been a difficult process in ensuring everyone's needs were met without compromising my own. Kia taught me there was an art to understanding and applying the science of parenting and teaching in my everyday life to maximize my time. Parenting and teaching doesn't have to be mutually exclusive. When you add children to any mix, you're eager to make sure you're aiding in their cognitive development and doing everything the right way. I felt my child only had one life so I had better get it right the first time. I couldn't paint a broad stroke over every issue but I had to find the art or life's clues in the proper context to prevent parenting from being so difficult for me.

This book not only signifies help, but gives you a glimpse of hope. It lets you know with every waking moment there is a skill that can be taught and it shows you the best way to teach it. There is an art to everything we do in life. As artists, we take what we have learned and make it our own. When I was a new mom, everything I did was for my son and with my son. His cognitive growth even in utero was a priority to me because I understood the early benefits of brain development. I adopted skills from all of the parenting books I read, all of the old-wives tales I inherited, and the do's and don'ts from friends and family to take ownership of my own parenting and learn my own style. I had to paint my own masterpiece because sometimes you'll realize you're going against what's popular.

This book will save you time in researching, reading and doing things the long, wrong way....simple, everyday considerations that we just don't think about to maximize our time. How many times have you wished your child came with instructions? And when you're concerned not only about your child's social and emotional development but their cognitive development as well, add another level of angst or take advantage of these foolproof methods. Whether new parents or seasoned, we're always looking for natural ways to make learning fun and this book shows us we can do just that.

Certainly, parenting can be a little heuristic here and there because what works for one child may not for the other and what worked for you, may not for me. In this book, however, are some universal truths that transcend cultures when it comes to parenting. This is a significant body of work for every new parent with children, especially young children from birth to adolescence. As founder of a local preschool and elementary school in SW Atlanta, I have seen the benefits of children admitted to our programs when they come with a basic set of essential skills. The lack thereof has had startling implications.

These tools are good for the children but definitely empowering for the parents. I'll leave you with one of my favorite quotes of all times by Eric Hoffer. Hoffer said, "In times of change learners inherit the earth; while the learned find themselves beautifully equipped to deal with a world that no longer exists." Keep learning, this is a great trait to pass on to your children. Today, you win...exponentially! - TJuani Bell Marks, MS/ Founder and Headmaster of OMNI International School, Atlanta GA

Introduction

Are you that Dad who is totally invested in teaching your daughter everything she needs to know about reading and math and your daughter is only two-years-old?

Are you that Mom who takes her baby to every meet-up, library read-aloud, science for toddlers, and language luncheon for littles program you can find?

Are you expecting a baby and while your understanding of parenthood isn't crystal clear, you do have ideas of what you want for your baby?

After having worked in many school settings, I will always remember a conversation I had with one parent whose child was about four-years-old when we met. Her daughter was behind her peers academically though she was a very smart little girl. Her Mom was very active in school. She was active with the parent committee. She did what was asked regarding help with homework. She was very involved and was always willing to help out. One day she came to me and shared that she had no idea that her daughter could possibly learn all that she had learned in the short time she had been attending the school. She went on to say, had she known that she should be teaching her some of those things at home, she would have. Let's say this Mom's name is Sheila. This book is for all of the Sheilas. This book is for the parents who did not know that their children were even capable of such unimaginable genius. This book is for the parents who have always known that their children were capable of greatness but want more ideas for unlocking their potential.

Let's start with the basics. People often ask my husband, Chinenye, and I if our children ever do anything wrong. Our response is usually something to the degree of, "They are children and they do regular stuff that regular children do. They are generally well-behaved children. They are also curious and are learning and growing, like all other children." Now, if you ever read about our children, even in teachable moments we are careful about what we say. Why? This tip is a freebie… Children have not asked to be on social media. They have not asked to be in books. They have not asked to be on websites. We are careful about what we say about our children because it was not their decision to post about themselves and we want them to be old enough to make decisions about posts that may otherwise be deemed embarrassing or cause for ammunition against them in their future lives. Now that we have that out of the way, let's get down to it!

Why keep reading a book from the lady my friend told me about? A quick bit about myself. I am Kia Haselrig-Oparah, mom of two, wife, daughter, sister and friend. I am a published author, Yum Yum! New Tastes are Fun! I also co-authored a book with my husband, "The Things I See: Scavenger Hunt," which is an activity book for children. By education and experience, I am a school psychologist, who is currently certified in three states though I am not currently working in that capacity. I was a school psychologist and worked with children from head start through high school. I have done in-home and community therapy. I have worked in a medical setting as a psychometrist, completing neuropsychological evaluations for people experiencing memory concerns - people with Alzheimer's, Dementia, Traumatic Brain Injury, Autism, and other Learning Challenges. In the nonprofit world, Chinenye and I worked as Youth Program Coordinators, providing leadership skills training and leading community service projects with middle and high school students. Chinenye is an engineer by education but has enjoyed teaching high school math and physics for the past seven years. Currently, I teach English to children in China; I am the owner of Raise the Bar Learning, LLC, which is an educational and parent consulting firm; and I am the COO of our daughter's business. I am also on the Board, as the Board of Directors of the school Kemery attended, where she learned most of the Japanese she knows now.

Our daughter is the 10-year old CEO of her company, Kemery Kreates. She started her business, per her request, to go to Japan when she and her classmates were invited by their teacher. Fluent in Japanese, she teaches Japanese Classes online through her Japanese Backpack course. She also teaches an entrepreneurship course that she created out of a desire to help other children follow their dreams and believe in themselves. This was sparked after she was included in a book collaboration and became a published author. She has a chapter in the book, *The Science Behind It: Formulating Success at Any Age.* Her business focuses on Connecting Cultures through Language, Fashion, and

Entrepreneurship. The fashion component is her clothing line, Kira by Kemery Kreates, which had 18 designs on the runway of Atlantic City Fashion Week in February 2018. Kemery learned to read when she was 2.5 years old and has been an avid reader ever since. She loves science and enjoys school. Kemery loves being outside, nature, and animals-especially horses. Kemery recently completed her 21st race, which was her 4th triathlon. She started learning Japanese at 13 months old. In addition to teaching classes online, she is now teaching her baby brother.

Our son is 2-years old, although he would tell you that he's "two-and-a-half. He loves everything his big sister is doing. He now wants to lead us in prayer - in Japanese - before eating! He recognizes all of the letters and knows the letter sounds. We recently began working with him on reading words and he is learning quickly. This little guy is loads of fun, like his sister! They both have quite a sense of humor too. They are kind to others and are fun to be around.

Would I say that all of the experience and having cool babies makes me a parenting expert? I'm not sure. Is there even such a thing? I do know children from a developmental and educational viewpoint. I have a passion for educating children that goes beyond what one may ever consider as traditional. One thing is certain, I can honestly say that parenting has been a fun experience for me and what that for other parents as well. Has it been work? Of course! No doubt about it! It has been the most fulfilling work of my life and I am thrilled to be on this parenting ride. The best part about what the experiences I have and the experiences

Chinenye and I share with our children is that we have witnessed in our home that there are some things that can be duplicated. Check this out though. We can duplicate the process. That does not necessarily mean we are duplicating the outcome? By duplicating many of the processes in our own home, we sometimes obtain different results. Be that as it may, the results have been good. The same rules apply when I worked in the school system as a school psychologist. We can implement the same intervention and sometimes get different results with different children. Why? Children are different and that's the beauty of who they are in that moment. I would suggest that we are all parenting experts to some extent because you are the expert of your own child. Nobody in the world knows your child better than you do unless they live with someone else on a regular basis.

Before we move on, please proceed with the expectation and understanding that every child is different and they learn at different paces. It's okay! I shared with you a bit about our experience and our children's strengths to let you know that you're reading from someone with professional experience and as well as personal experience - not as a point of comparison. Even our two children are very different. We celebrate differences! We have two friends who both have children who have autism. One friend is a single Mom and the other friend is married. Both Moms put in time with their sons and it shows! The point is that this resource is available with the understanding that we are striving for our child's own best potential. Each child has strengths and weaknesses that are different from another child and that is wonderful!

One thing we know for sure is that parenting at this level is intentional. Parenting requires effort, action and sometimes even strategy, which is why I say parenting is a verb. The goal is to make learning fun! When learning is fun, children never want to stop learning!

No stress. No progress comparisons. No disappointment for effort.

Praise. Fun learning. Encouragement. Exposure to information.

All that being said, let's Raise the Bar on Learning!

Contents

Chapter 1

Mindset

Let's start with the mindset that from the time a child has ears and a brain, they can begin learning. There are different schools of thought on how much learning takes place in utero. Chinenye and I did not do much research on this. We used what we know, what we believed, and took a stance on the idea that if the baby has ears and a brain is forming, then we can start teaching. What does that look like in utero? In general, we are usually a peaceful family. We were more cognizant about what we said. We were cautious about the type of energy we were around, meaning we chose to be around positive people. We played more peaceful music. I will say that sometimes my radio talk show of choice may not have been contrary to the plan; however, that was the exception, not the norm.

Truth be told, I began being very intentional about parenting before I was even married. I became radical in my thinking about what I did to my body, the place where my future baby would grow. I was never much for alcohol, though I would have a drink every now and then. I stopped perming my hair and laid off the constant nail polish to cut back on the chemicals that my body was exposed to regularly. At the time, I was doing better with my food choices and I worked out fairly regularly. This part has been a struggle for me since entering adulthood. It's still about being intentional. Yes, this is drastic and I am not suggesting that everyone has to go this far. I am suggesting that when deciding to have a baby, start becoming intentional about your approach to having a baby, growing a baby, loving a baby, and teaching a baby.

There are also different schools of thought about what to teach children and when. I'm going to share with you the approach that Chinenye and I chose for our children. This is not a book of judgment about how you choose to parent. It's your choice. This is not a right or wrong kind of discussion. We often get asked about our children and the truth is that we have always been willing to share with those who are interested in hearing our journey. I hope that you gain something from this book that will help you on your parenting journey.

Before moving forward with this book, let's open our hearts and minds to receive the notion that all children can learn. Let's agree that children learn at different paces and that's okay. Let's challenge ourselves to not set limits on what children can learn. We can go one step further and embrace the idea that once we have decided to not set limits on what children can learn, we will release the grip of the "average" timeline of when a skill should be learned. The guidelines are good. Let's let them remain guidelines and not stay stuck on the idea that a child can only learn a skill at a certain age. Now that all hearts and minds are clear, let's unlock your baby's potential!

Chapter 2

* princess ornament*

Identifying Family

When a baby is born, they are charged with learning numerous skills, seemingly all at once. It's a big deal learning to nurse, open their eyes, hold their head up, and otherwise communicate their needs. Aside from the beginner baby stuff, one of the first things that we worked on with our children is recognizing the people who live in our home and are in our family. This is not an overnight skill. It takes time and is an ongoing process, as we add new family members to the list. The goal was to bring about familiarity to ease the transition when our sweet babies met new members of the family. What are some ways to work on this skill?

Activity 1: From the time our baby was born, we would hold her, look her in the eyes and say something simple like, "Mommy sees Kemery. Does Kemery see Mommy?" At some point, the recognition will be there. As your baby is able to turn their head more independently, the game becomes more interesting and you can ask, "Where's Grandmommy?" as they look around the room for her.

Activity 2: This is one of few times we will advocate for technology with a teeny baby but what a great way for family members, separated by miles, to connect with your little one. Plan video chats. As your little one gets older, they will get used to giving Grandaddy a few minutes of their time to chat, hear each other's voice and connect. This actually has become a very special tool in our family. When Kemery was very small, we were able to arrange for her meet her Great-Grandmother online, in Nigeria, before she died! She was able to sing songs for her talk with her. What special moments! Also, she has been able to maintain relationships with her Grandparents, aunts, uncles, and cousins all by using video chats to connect. When we see family in person, it is like we never missed a beat. Actually, now, Kemery has suggested weekly family calls and the family was all for it. Every week family can chime in for about 20 minutes to debrief about the week from wherever they may be in the world. Since implementing the family calls this year, we have had family members chime in from Georgia, Ohio, Canada, North Carolina, the Great Lakes, Maryland, Nigeria, and France!

Activity 3: When our daughter was a baby, we found a little baby photo album. The handle was a teether and everything! It was literally a baby safe photo album. All we did was put in pictures of Mommy, Daddy, Aunts, Uncles, first cousins, and Grandparents. We did it in families, which made for more fun when she was old enough to look at a family and "point to Uncle B" or "find Grandpa."

Chapter 3

❧❦

Name Song

Here's another activity that can start as soon as your baby is born but is not too late to start if your baby does not already have this skill mastered. Make up a song that includes your baby's first, middle, and last name. The song should include the correct pronunciation (no curly cues or riffs in the middle of your child's first name unless you want it pronounced like that) and then break down the spelling of each name. The best part is that there is no right or wrong way to accomplish this task. We literally used the tune of Twinkle Twinkle Little Star or the Alphabet Song (you do know this is the same tune, right?) for our daughter's name. We added some variation for her name at the end of the song and a little in the middle.

For our son, his song was completely made up. We are not songwriters. We did not enlist the help of a professional. We wanted it to be a special song for each of them, that we could actually sing. We started singing their name songs to them when they were infants. Sing the name song to your baby every day, multiple times a day, if you want. What's really special about the name song is that it is unique to your baby. Given that you made it up, there is nobody else, probably in the world, who would have the same name song.

Your baby's name song may become a comfort song. This may be the song that helps stop the tears in a stressful baby moment. Maybe not but it will always be nostalgic when it is brought up over Thanksgiving dinner in 15 years. Additionally, it will help your little one to become familiar with how to spell their name. Both of our children could spell their first, middle, and last names when they were two-years-old. Remember, this should be fun. This is not a competition. This should not be stressful. If your child does not learn to spell their name until they are three or four-years-old, don't panic. Children learn at different paces. The song is only one technique you can use to help with spelling. As your children get older, you will also want them to see their name in writing to allow them to associate the letters in the song to the letters in print. Reading to your child, playing word games, identifying letters and sounds, etc. All of these strategies, together, will help you to unlock your child's genius. The name song is one fun way you can begin this process from birth.

Chapter 4

Stop Singing the Alphabet

Hear me out on this one. I am a huge fan of teaching information through songs. I would argue that the alphabet song is not as helpful as the introduction to learning the alphabet, UNLESS, you stop singing it the way it was taught to us. There is no letter el-em-in-oh-pee. For our daughter, we did not sing the alphabet to her until she could say the letters of the alphabet, in order. Well, when we sang the song, we slowed it down and enunciated very clearly to allow her to hear the different letters between L-P. After she could tell us the letters and we knew she was solid in her understanding, we introduced the song, pointing out to her that we pronounce each of the letters. Is this dramatic? Maybe. For us, this worked.

Let me emphasize this point. If we want our children to speak well, read well, and spell well we have to give them every opportunity for exposure to proper grammar, speech, and pronunciation. It will not happen at the same time for every child. However, we increase our likelihood of expediting this process by exposing our children to the information they need to be successful.

We did not engage in baby talk with our children. That does not mean that we talked to our baby's with an adult tone. We chose not to reinforce the incorrect pronunciation of words. I must admit that there were a few words that both Kemery said and Jeremy says that we let them say a few times before correcting them because it sounded too cute to correct. Guilty as charged. Even those words were corrected at some point though. By-in-large, we stuck to the plan of speaking the way we want our children to read, write, and speak.

Chapter 5

Increase Vocabulary

According to the Georgia Early Education Alliance for Ready Students (2018), "There are approximately 2000 days from when a child is born to when a child starts pre-school. During the first 2,000 days, our brains grow fastest between the ages of 0 and 3."

Increasing vocabulary is another skill we worked on even before birth. We really ramped things up after birth though. How'd we do it? Okay, truth is that this is integrated into so many different aspects of learning that there's no way we'd cover it all in this chapter, or even this book. Here's our basic approach. This is a good one. Lean in close. Closer. Closer. Okay, ready? Talk. I know, right? So simple yet not such a common approach, it seems. Think about this, children learn from what they see, hear, and do. Turn the television off. I know, it's such an easy fix sometimes. Turn the television off and talk. Yes, to the baby too. Put that bouncy near you (always in a safe place) and explain to your baby what you are doing. What do I talk about? They don't understand yet. Guess what? You weren't born understanding either. The more your talk, the more they hear. This is when they are learning about sentence structure, the flow of speech, conversations, intonation, etc. There is so much being learned simply by listening to you talk! Unless you know that your speech is worse than what they would learn from television, turn the tv off and let them learn how to speak appropriately, from you.

One thing to remember though is that we do not always talk properly. Why? It's not necessary to talk to your significant other with proper grammar at all times. It may be a little weird sometimes. However, with our children, we chose to be more particular about how we speak in front of here. Who cares? She's was only one-year-old or three-years-old, right? Not so much. Consider this. If I pronounced the word, library as "library," when I teach my toddler to sound out words for spelling, what do you think would happen? If she listens to me repeatedly tell my husband, "I'm 'bout to go to libary," how do you think she would spell the word, "about," or the word, "library," when it was time to learn to spell those words? Are you with me? Is this too much? Is this really a thing? I never did the research on it specifically but it's certainly one piece of advice I gave to families whose children struggled with spelling when I was a school psychologist. I must add that it is tougher than you think, to always be aware of what you are saying. Sometimes Chinenye and I would check each other, which is a good thing. Be gentle in checking each other and never in front of the children though. Remember, this should not be a stressful process. It should; however, be intentional. Did this strategy work? For us, it did. Kemery placed in every spelling be she ever participated in - two first-place ribbons, one second-place ribbon, and one third place ribbon.

How do you talk to a baby who doesn't talk back? This is tricky. For this one, you have to trust the process. Explain what you are doing. Instead of going to make a sandwich and coming back with a prepared sandwich, give the details of what you are doing, when you are doing it. Talk about the ingredients, talk about the materials and kitchen utensils being used and talk about the process of making the sandwich. Then, you could talk about how it tastes. Speak the way you want your baby to speak. If you want to hear "goo-goo" and "ga-ga," then go for it. Somehow, I suspect you are not reading *this* book with *that* goal in mind.

Chapter 6

❧✦(ᴄᴏ)✦❧

Time to Sign

How do you teach a baby sign language? For every word you know a sign for, use it every time you say that word, starting from the time your baby is born. Babies learn through exposure and repetition. When you talk to your baby, use the signs you know. Don't know sign language? Use your resources. Go online. Check out a book at the library. Take one of those classes that some libraries offer for Parent and Me signing classes. Ask a friend to teach you some. Chances are that you know somebody who knows enough to get you by. There are numerous benefits of making the effort and taking the time to teach your baby to sign. Some of the words we taught our children were: please, thank you (yes, even nonverbal babies can use manners), mom, dad, grandma, grandpa, milk, water, eat and more.

Using sign language is tricky. How so? We have to be careful because some children will rely so heavily on sign language that they will choose not to speak if they know how or not put the same effort into learning to speak because they have an alternate method of communication. This was not the case with either of our children yet I still remind you to remain cautious and aware of signs that your baby is favoring signing over speaking.

Okay, now that I've said that, let me get into a few more benefits of using sign language. Our goal is to increase communication and decrease frustration. This helps everyone involved. Using even the most basic signs, like the ones I've mentioned earlier, helps tremendously. Many times, children are crying because they lack the skills necessary to articulate their needs. Think about it. If for some reason, you could not speak for a certain amount of time yet you had a need to go to the restroom or you already used the restroom on yourself, wouldn't you have a sense of urgency to get the help you need to rectify that situation? If you were hungry and you could not tell someone you need food, how would you get their attention? Let's throw in the fact that you can't walk either? As a matter of fact, you have no idea how to get your hands to create the drink or food that you need to satisfy your hunger? How would you address that? Truthfully, have you ever been out at an all-day meeting and you left your lunch, you stayed up way too late working on your presentation, you had to do task after task until you are so exhausted that you sit there on the verge of tears, in hopes that you can grab a bite to eat and simply crawl into your bed to get some rest? This has happened to you at least once, right? If this happens to us as adults, think about the littlest members of our family who have not even begun to learn to regulate their emotions at such an advanced level.

Sign language is not a cure for frustration. However, it is a tool that we can use to lessen the frustration for both parents and babies.

Chapter 7

Skip the Pronouns

There are various research studies available that reveal children from homes with a lower socioeconomic status hear half as many words as children from families with a higher socioeconomic status. The statistics are alarming. The most challenging part for me is that words are free. It makes sense that the quality of word may be impacted. However, in keeping with the idea that we can give our children the best of what we have to offer, if children need to hear words in order to increase their vocabulary, it's worth the sacrifice to spend time talking with them about many different experiences and topics.

In an effort to increase vocabulary, let's ditch pronouns for a while. What do I mean? You could tell your daughter, "Bring me that, over there," while you're pointing at what you want her to bring you or you could say, "Layla, please bring Mommy your pink blanket." You have now increased from using five unique words to using seven unique words and the seven words are also more meaningful words to a young child learning vocabulary. You could say, "Get down" or you could say, "Devin, Daddy wants you to put your feet on the floor so you won't get hurt. You can play with your toy car or your piano instead." Wow! We took a two-word sentence to two sentences with twenty-six words. Does this take more time? Yes. Is this more work? Yes. Is it worth it? Yes. It does not cost one dime to increase your child's vocabulary if you are willing to put in the work. It's challenging at first but the exponential benefits your child gains by your intentional effort is all the reward you need to make it worth it.

Chapter 8

※❦(ᴄᴄ)❦※

Body Parts

One of the first things we taught both of our children is their body parts. Besides the obvious, Heads, Shoulders, Knees and Toes Song, knowing body parts serves many other purposes. Whether you choose to homeschool or not, at some point your children will leave your home and be in the care of somebody else. As our pastor would say, "I wish somebody would know where I'm going and meet me there." One of the things I need my children to have the ability to tell me is about injuries and in attempts or talk of inappropriate touch or requests. Assuming the best and not the worst, we'll leave the obvious serious nature of the latter for later discussion (though it's necessary to have been stated) and let's focus on injuries. If a child is bleeding, vomiting, or has diarrhea these are obvious signs that they are not feeling well or something has happened. What happens when there is an earache, tummy ache, headache, or a sore vagina? *GASP* Did she just use the v-word? Yes. Yes, she did. Why? The first reason is that it is accurate. If you use the correct terminology with your child, you know what they are referring to and if you hear them use another "pet name" for that body part, you can begin to question where they learned that information. What if it hurts when your toddler is urinating or having a bowel movement?

When you can trust your child to give you an accurate account of injuries, you can begin to address the concern and you eliminate the wasted time of guessing to figure out what's wrong. Knowing what area to target intervention is key to prompt attention and to ease your child's pain or discomfort.

Let's take it a step farther. Approach learning body parts like learning a new language. Our one-year-old niece can name her body parents in English and in Igbo. When Kemery was one-year-old, she could name her body parts in multiple languages. Our son has two-names for many of his body parts. Children are generally hard-wired with the ability to receive multiple languages in a special way that becomes exponentially more challenging as we become adults. As such, this is a great time for children to learn more information simply by exposing them to those resources.

For example, let's assume children have no knowledge of the body parts when born yet it's expected they can easily learn eyes, nose, ears, mouth, toes, fingers, stomach, etc. Following me? Okay, why then would we not expect that they can learn scapula, clavicle, Achilles tendon, phalanges, patella, knuckles, heels, elbows, etc.? We have to be radical in our thinking if we want to maximize the potential in our children, the potential that already exists yet goes untapped because we didn't believe they could or needed to learn it yet. Let's Raise the Bar on Learning!

Chapter 9

※~⁀⟨ᴄᴏ⟩⁀~※

Emotions

Consider the possibility of equipping your children with what they need to communicate at a basic level such that the need for tears becomes of minimal necessity. Don't get me wrong, we can't eliminate tears completely, nor would we want to do that because they are a natural part of being a healthy, emotionally stable human being. For a baby or a young child, tears are mostly due to the inability to effectively communicate their needs. When we empower our little ones with the ability to communicate their feelings, we open up an entire world of communication possibilities for them and for you as well.

How do we do this? Remember the goal is for fun learning. There are lots of ways to practice connecting with emotions. You can grab a book and look through the pages and talk about how the characters look and how they might feel.

When we get to the point of reading stories together, we can ask more in-depth questions about how characters might feel in different situations.

Living in the age of technology abundance, selfies with a cell phone camera are a fun way to practice making different faces and tying the faces into different emotions. Remember to keep the technology to a minimum, though, because they won't have a difficult time jumping into that world soon enough but it's a fun way to switch up learning.

Grab a mirror and practice making faces. Go for the basics first like happy, sad, and mad. Easy, right? Great! Now, let's add to that by digging into other emotions like frustrated, tired, scared, surprised, and hurt. Funny thing is that if you practice these faces, they may not nail it the way you and I know the emotion to look on others (not right away); however, you will know what their version of this emotion looks like on them. You will have a starting point of asking questions when the emotion begins to be used in an appropriate context.

Seriously. Here's an example: Our son was going through a phase of being very upset. He was two-years-old, which, to me, means he was being normal, right? However, we wanted to figure out how to work through what he was experiencing to decrease the amount of time he had to struggle with that feeling. Literally, this happened. One day, he was so upset. I went in, sat with him, and talked. I told him that I can see he is very upset and I want him to calm down to tell me what is bothering him. I'm not lying. I was really having a discussion with a two-year-old. They are capable of this level of communication if we teach them the skills. I told him that I felt sad when he was sad and I wanted to help him feel happy. He told me that I was not sad because I was not crying. At that moment, almost on cue, I cried. Not an ugly cry but I could not hold back the frustration I was having by not being able to calm him down and get to the bottom of his issue, especially at the end of a very long day and evening. I don't usually cry in front of my children. Some say that's good and some say that's not good but it's just me. That moment, he was crying and I was crying. I hugged him and told him that you don't have to cry to be sad but I was very sad because I wanted to help him.

At that moment, he began to calm down. I held him and he began to calm down. This was the start of our conversation. I asked him if he was mad. He said, "No." Sad? "No." Angry? "No." Happy? "No." I paused because I was unsure if he was going to give me an answer other than, "No," if I should keep asking or just accept the calming for what it was worth and call it a night. I pushed a little further and asked, "What's wrong? How are you feeling?" He looked straight ahead for a moment, paused, and then looked at me. In the calm, sweet voice, he said, "I feel frustrated." I was stunned. My father-in-law tells Chinenye and I that we teach our babies these words and concepts and then are surprised when they use them.

Here's another quick story. Our little guy was sick. He had Hand-Foot-Mouth Disease. He picked it up at school and fortunately, he must have had the mildest case ever. Thank goodness for that! He sat calmly in the chair in our room. He wasn't quite the same energetic little guy we're used to but he didn't look like a toddler who was sick. I asked him how he was feeling and he again surprised me by responding, "I'm comfortable." My father-in-law was right. We teach our children these things and are surprised when they use them. Raise the Bar on Learning!

Chapter 10

Teach Them to Listen to Their Body

Now that your children know their body parts and can express their emotions, you're smooth sailing, right? Not exactly. They are still children who are learning to navigate those feelings. One thing you want to learn to do is to be an observer of behavior. There are two types of communication - verbal and nonverbal. Both forms of communication can be effective ways of sharing a message with a listener or receiver of information; although, verbal and nonverbal communication often work better together.

Here's a story about our daughter. Generally, Kemery had always been very well-behaved. There was a time when Kemery was younger and was working on consequences for behavior. It seems like every so often her behavior was very unusual. Even her Worst Behavior wasn't really out of control; however, we wanted to be diligent in correcting behavior and teaching appropriate behavior early on. On those rare occasions where her behavior became unruly, naturally, the consequences would increase. We started noticing a pattern. It seems like whenever her behavior was unusual, it would be followed by illness. Of course, the first few times we felt horrible but how would we know that she was on her way to be sick? As a person who studies behavior, we soon realized that this was the pattern. Her very young self had no other way to communicate to us that she felt bad.

I'm not saying that unruly behavior should go without consequences. I bring this up as a way to shed light on the various ways that our little ones communicate with us. Once we realized that her behavior usually was indicative out, we addressed the behaviors differently. For her, the behaviors were our sign that we need to look at how she's feeling, take note of temperature, activeness, or other indicators that she may not be feeling well. Without fail, unruly behaviors led to pink eye, ear infections and even pneumonia. Ironically, this pattern does tend to be the same for our son. It won't be the same for all children but if you get nothing else from this section of the book, begin to practice understanding your child's behavior. Look at what happens before they do something that gets them into trouble or what happens after they do something that gets them into trouble.

Here's one that many people would disagree with me about but that's cool. Everybody won't go about parenting in the same way, and that's okay. I hope I'm not the only one who does this but I do it. Let me start with an example. If I forgot to put moisturizer on my toddler's mouth and know they usually have dry lips, I'll go the entire day without using any chapstick or lip gloss. Why would I do that? Once I have experienced something, like have dry lips, I am more likely to more thoughtful to my baby's needs in the future.

While we are on the topic of teaching our children to listen to their body, it's important that we give them permission to listen to protect their body and listen to their emotions as well. Teach your children that they have the right to tell people not to touch their body, even grown-ups. Please give them permission and encourage them to be firm in their stance when they say they do not want to be tickled, even by grown-ups. Hugs are optional. Maybe a high-five, fist bump, or wave accompanied by a verbal greeting will be sufficient. Teaching children to listen to their instinct is a tricky thing but it's necessary. Speaking of tricky, I was advised to stop talking about stranger danger and to start talking about tricky people. Making this switch became important as we learned that many times in life, we may need the assistance of a stranger but we may need to avoid the unwanted advances of a family member or friend. Helping children to navigate the difference between tricky people and strangers will help them to listen to their instincts and what they've learned about other people to hopefully make more informed decisions about who is safe and whom we should take caution. It is good for children to know how to establish and stand firm in their boundaries.

Chapter 11

Be Observant and Empathetic

For a brief moment, I questioned whether or not I should actually put this in writing. I decided to go ahead and write it in hopes that it helps someone else the way it has helped me. If this is not for you, no worries. As I have landed the role of Mommy, one of the ways I seek to understand my children's needs better is to consider how I would feel if I were in their shoes. Even at the most basic level, I seek to understand their world. For example, toddlers who are not yet talking may not be able to say that their lips are chapped and they would like some Chapstick for their mouth. When I go to apply Chapstick to comfort my own lips, I do a quick scan to see if my children are in need of that same assistance (when they are old enough for this - not referring to babies). You see? I told you, some of you may judge me for this but I do what works for me and that's all I hope for you as well - do what works for you.

Here are other examples. This part is out of our control but I am adding this short section of the book to help you to become an observer of your behavior and your child's behavior as well. I often wonder about whether stars aligned perfectly or if there is Divine Intervention somehow with some of the ways I connect to understand what my children are going through. I never had asthma growing up and I did not get it until I had a child who was diagnosed with asthma. I'm not saying I'm excited to have asthma or that this is a great way to connect. I do appreciate being able to understand her in a different way. I never had such an exhausting of allergies until I became an adult, after having a child with allergies. I understand her better now.

I'll let this be a short chapter regarding what happens in Divine Order for the sake of understanding but I will encourage you to think about how you are feeling and take even a brief moment to consider, is my child feeling that way too? Dad's or Mom's with short haircuts, if your hair itches when it needs to be cut, consider that your toddler (once haircuts start to happen) may be itchy too when their hair begins to grow back. If your skin is dry, check with your little one to see how their skin is feeling. Most parents are already attentive to their children. I am bringing up the idea of being in tune with what your little one may need but may not be able to communicate yet.

Also, consider this. Have you ever had a bad day? What do you do to move on past that moment? Do you workout at the gym? Do you have lunch with the guys? Do you take a mental health day and hit the spa by yourself or with your girlfriends? Do you take some alone time to sit in your favorite chair and read a book for 20 minutes? How do children decompress when they have a bad day? Rather, do we even give them the opportunity to own that feeling and have a way to release those feelings in a healthy way or do we add to their stress? If your child has a bad day, do we then fuss at them about cleaning their room? Moving too slowly? Not looking at you when you speak to them? Not starting their homework right away?

This is a work in progress for me. Sometimes Chinenye and I have to check each other when we are being "too much" for the moment that our child is experiencing at that time. Children need to know that they are allowed to have feelings, own those feelings, and be given an opportunity to work through those feelings. I am not suggesting giving them license to run the house with their bad attitude. I am suggesting being observant. Asking if they need to talk before heading up to take their shower (for older children). Giving some hug and maybe story time together before insisting that they pick up their toys. Maybe they need some alone time to calm down before they can talk about it and before we start a new task. They may need you to change your tone because like we tell them, it's not what you say. It's how you say it.

Chapter 12

Model Behavior

I'll teach you one of the phrases that have worked for me in the past. If Kemery was having a rough time and began to raise her voice, I would calmly ask her if she wanted to make her tone match mine or if she wanted me to make my tone match hers. I would tell her that the choice was hers. One hundred percent of the time, she made the right choice. That leads me into empty threats. After working with children for many years, I have learned that threatening consequences and not following through is a mistake that many adults make. As silly as it sounds, telling your child that they are in for a consequence that is not even realistic, like knocking them into next week, is not helpful. Saying you are going to take away their cell phone when you really bought it for your own peace of mind and convenience, meaning you have no intention of taking it away, is not helpful. If you overuse consequences, they do not work. If you suggest consequences and never follow through, they don't work. Use consequences sparingly; only when really necessary. Generally speaking, we aim to operate in a system of rewards because children respond better to praise.

When we do opt for consequences, rather, interventions, our hope is that they are meaningful and not punitive. Here's a buzzword that may send parents running for the hills. Time-out. Many people are against time-out. As I think about this more deeply, I am content with the idea that we can all use a break from time-to-time. Sometimes we need to take a moment for ourselves to reflect on what happened. Why would children be any different? If we opted for a time-out with our little ones, we prepared them before with what they need to think about while they are sitting there. What information do we want them to process and reflect on before being able to return to playing. Also, we don't leave them there for long periods of time. They likely wouldn't even remember what they did to get themselves there in the first place, if we left them for too long.. Some researcher decided that one minute for each year of the child's age would be sufficient. For example, a four-year-old could handle four minutes of reflection. We used that as our starting point. For us, those minutes may start over if they were not quiet during that time. After time was up, it was important to review what they did (or didn't do), brainstorm ways to avoid this situation again in the future and encourage them to make good choices in the future.

As Kemery got older, our interventions were more creative. One time, she really did something. I'm not even sure what it was anymore. I removed all books and toys from her room. I created a book of motivational quotes. Each quote was assigned points based on the length and complexity of the quote. She was given a reasonable time frame to learn as many quotes as she could to earn back the things she wanted to join her back in her room. It also helped us to clean out her room because she chose what was important to her by earning those items back first. It's a win-win for everyone! Beyond that, now it has been years and Kemery still enjoys looking through the quote book and we pick a quote on the way to school to get our day started on the right track. What started out as a consequence was really designed as an educational resource. This could backfire if you have a child who does not like reading because you have now made reading a punishment by associating it with something bad. For her, she loves to read and since we had all of her books, I think she secretly enjoyed learning the quotes and felt challenged to learn more in order to earn some of her things back before the rest were donated. There was no fussing or yelling involved with the presentation of the quote book. It was a means to learn and to earn back her things. We have a friend, she and her husband are all into dishing out creative interventions for her sons. For them, they get the desired results every time. Consequence turned into a reward. Yes, it's more work. They are worth it. Get creative!

Chapter 13

꧁꧂

It's All in the Approach

We're often asked about how polite are and appreciative our children, especially Kemery since she is older and more people have experience with her thoughtfulness. I'm going to reveal the secret. Ready? It's all in the approach. From the time Kemery and Jeremy were both little, we made it our business to bring out the enthusiasm for every gift or every experience. Let's take a look at this scenario:

Parent: I brought you something. (Notice, I said brought and not bought. Having appreciation is not surrounded around material items and certainly is not necessarily connected to newly purchased items either.)

Child: What is it?

Parent: Let me get it. I think you're going to love it. It's your favorite color!

Child: I want to see. What is it?

Parent: We got you your very own shiny pencil! It's a sparkly pencil. Do you want to hold it?

Child: Oooooh, I love it! Thank you!

Sound corny? Well, this is pretty much what happened when I brought home new pencils. When you give someone something with enthusiasm in your voice and expression, they will most likely love it as much as you do, if you raise them this way, and condition them to respond in this way. Think about it, if you focus on the importance of relationships, from birth, and teach your child the importance of appreciating experiences and valuing the gesture over the amount; you are setting your little one up for success. Happiness isn't in how big something is or how much something costs.

Being mindful of your approach is helpful in other ways too. Here's another example: Let's say your toddler is not interested in moving on to the next task. If you offer something else and you offer it in a way that is undeniably amazing, who could refuse that offer? Remember, children can see through transparent. You have to be sincere. Show genuine enthusiasm for what you give and the suggestions you offer. In turn, your toddler will be more appreciative.

Still not convinced? Add this to the mix…give your toddler choices? Say what? Are you kidding? They are only children. They should do as I say because I said it. We've heard this before and have maybe even said it ourselves. Well, this is certainly one approach and while I agree to an extent, I contend that you and your child may have a more peaceful experience if you were speaking the same language. Your little one wants to have control. We all know who the adult is here though, right? As the adult, know when to pick your battles. Choices can be offered such that all roads lead back to what you wanted your little one to do in the first place. In doing this, it is actually empowering and guiding your child in making good choices. It's a win-win, for the most part.

Chapter 14

It's About Perspective

I'm certain you have heard of the "Terrible Twos," right? Have you ever considered the alternative? What if they were the "Terrific Twos?" That's exactly the approach we have taken with both of our children. People have different beliefs about the power of words. What if it were true that what you put out in the universe is what you will get back? If you believe that your two-year-old will be terrible, wouldn't it be easier for that to be true? Make sense, right? We were determined not to have the terrible two phase take hold of our home. Again, it's not that our children did nothing wrong because we "willed" them not to do it. We believed in their inherent ability to learn what we teach them. Given that they were born with brains and born with ears, we thought we had a good starting point to "reason" with a two-year-old. I don't give professional psychology advice when I'm not working as a psychologist. I will say that behavior takes time to change and it often gets worse before it gets better when applying an intervention. Our goal was to work on prevention and avoid the need for intervention. In some ways that worked and in other ways, we had to be more creative and think of alternatives. Who knew you could reason with two-year-olds? When you put in the work on the front end, it's a lot easier because they are prepared to utilize the reasoning skills you've been teaching all along.

How do you prepare a one-year-old to avoid the terrible twos? Lean in close. Pat yourself on the back for buying this book and saving yourself from many tears (theirs and yours). There will still be tears but we can do our best to decrease these frustrating moments. Okay, are you ready? The way you prepare a one-year-old to avoid the terrible twos is by equipping them with the ability to communicate their needs, learn how to pick your battles, give choices where all roads lead to what you want them to do yet let them feel independent, remember they are people with feelings and do this all in a loving way. Sounds pretty complicated, right? Not really. It does take effort. It does take patience. It does take consistency.

Think about how you feel when you are told what to do or how you feel when you think something was not fair. Think about how you feel when you are being requested (or told) to do something when you don't feel well. You are now an adult. Consider how long it took you to learn how to regulate and manage your feelings. Truth be told, some of us are still working on wrapping our minds around how to handle our feelings. Imagine how challenging it must be to be two-years-old and being responsible for having to learn so much, so fast. Imagine being a 10-year-old who has to navigate hormones, friendships, academics, and her parents too. Give them a pass every so often. Pick your battles.

Chapter 15

Avoid the, "No!"

ere's another one that will make you feel like a genius for picking up this great book. I'm about to drop some top secret type of knowledge. Okay, it's not a secret but it sure seems to stump a lot of parents. Hopefully, I'm not speaking too soon, given our youngest is only two-year-old and still has time to prove me wrong. I hope that won't be the case though. Here's the real, "No" knowledge that you've been waiting to hear. If you want your baby to use a word other than, "No," you've got to stop using that word with them. I know. You were probably expecting something a little deeper than that, right? Well, I hate to break it to you but this is true. Children repeat what they hear, right? If you are telling your girl, "No," every five minutes, she's doing to get good at repeating you.

What do you do when you feel like a "No" is in order? Think to yourself, "Is this an emergency?" If the answer is, "yes" then please respond immediately with whatever needs to be said, which is usually a quick, "No!" Then, once safety is no longer a concern, address the safety issue with a child-friendly explanation of why what they were doing was potentially dangerous, what could happen if they continued to do what they were doing, and some options for what is acceptable to do in place of the behavior we are avoiding. If you do this often enough when they are very young (ages one and two), they will begin to be able to walk through this thought process with you walking you through the steps and allowing them to answer. Ultimately, we expect that they will begin to have this thought process more independently as they get older.

If it is not an emergency and you want your son to stop doing what he was doing or what he was about to do, think of what you could say instead of "No." This is the part that becomes problematic for many parents. This part requires effort and intentional decision to put in the time required to think through this process and not react with the first thing to comes to mind but to be thoughtful in our response. Here are some things you could say, instead of saying, "No." (1) May I go outside? (A) Today is not a good day because it's raining outside. For younger children, you could offer suggestions of what they could do instead. For older children, you could ask them for suggestions of what they could do instead. (2) Your daughter wants to brush her own teeth but you know she won't do it the way you want her to do it. (A) You could respond by thanking her for taking the initiative to brush her teeth. Let her know that she can brush her teeth independently after she helps you brush them first. (3) Your son is climbing on the kitchen stool. (A) Put your feet on the floor. You may not climb on the stool. Then, go through the steps of helping him understand why he should not climb on the stool.

Did this method completely eliminate the "No" phase for our children? In a word, "No." We thought we made it with both children. However, they both picked it up from school. I will say that it was a temporary phase for both of our children. We remained consistent at home and communicated our concern at school. The phase did not last more than a couple of weeks for either of our children. This is a hard concept to get behind because it requires quite a bit of effort and intentionality on the part of the parent. However, it is rewarding in numerous ways. In addition to avoiding the nagging, "No" phase, this method also increases vocabulary. The more words children hear, naturally, the more words they will learn over time.

Chapter 16

❦

Be Forgiving

This may be somewhat of an oxymoron. Who should be forgiven? The children or the parents? What do I mean by that? Take in this story. Chinenye and I agree that if we never taught our children not to do something and then they do it, then it is our own fault. That being said, we have become fairly good at being proactive and looking at the situation for what might happen before it actually happens and then being proactive in our teaching. Kemery was very young, maybe three- or four-years-old. At the time, we had someone coming to the house to watch her while I went to work. One day, I came home from work and I was greeted with an urgent apology from a certain little girl. She was talking fast and nervously. I asked her to explain why she was apologizing. She took me to the newly painted wall where she drew a big beautiful circle as long and wide as her little arm could reach. Fortunately,

Chinenye came home at that very moment. I passed the baton. I needed that cool down time because I was upset at myself for not being more proactive this one. We had talked about how we are supposed to write on paper, how we do not write on floors, we do not write on the table, etc. I don't remember covering the part about not writing on walls. Although I'm fairly certain she had a good understanding about what we could write on and what we could not write on, we never actually confirmed that she knew not to write on a wall and at that age, we could assume transference occurred but we could not confirm that with certainty. This has been a very rare occurrence with either of our children; however, it is worthy to note because it happens.

The point is that children are curious. They are explorers. They want to discover the world around them. They are going to mess up. Before you are quick to reprimand them, think about how much of what they have done is my own fault for not informing them they cannot do what they have done. This does not mean children can do whatever they want because you did not tell them not to do it. Children need discipline and structure. Be mindful of how being proactive can set the stage for successful exploration and decrease frustration for you and your child.

Chapter 17

Keep Moving!
Don't Stop Now!

How many times have we praised a child for counting from 1-10? Many times, right? Why? That's impressive that your one-year-old can count to 10! What happens after 10 though? Do move on to teaching something else? What's the reason? Was your goal to teach 1-10? What is the significance of 10? What if we kept counting? If your Jamal can count to 10, sure he can count to 15 or maybe even 35 if we did not put any limitations on what he could learn. What's hard to conceptualize is why we would even need a one-year-old to count to 35. My challenge to that is to think about the importance of counting to 10. It seems that somewhere along the way, we were taught that 10 was the magic stop number and I would argue that there's not a great reason that we would stop counting there. Let this be heard loud and clear, though: the goal is not to stress our babies to learning to the point of Avogadro's constant. We are simply exposing them to the information and if they get it, great! If not, that's great too!

I had amazing school experiences growing up. I was in the talented and gifted program throughout school and graduated from a science and technology program at the high school level. When I talk to Chinenye about his school experiences, he also had great experiences growing up. It's interesting that as an engineer, I think he would have really enjoyed the classes I had at my high school like architectural drafting and other technology classes. I wonder what my experiences would have been like in different settings. I remember having an hour-long school bus ride to attend middle school because they wanted me to go to great schools. I am happy with the path my parents chose for me regarding education. For the record, my husband and I both went to public schools. Our daughter has had a mix of public and private school experiences. We are advocates of education. Great educational experiences can happen in various settings.

My first experience outside of being in the classroom as a student and viewing education from an educator's viewpoint was when I was in college. I volunteered at an independent school. It was during an election year and the children were learning about the election process. The day I witnessed a three-year-old boy stand behind a podium and deliver his speech on why they should vote for him for Vice-

President of the school, was the day that my mind was all the way opened to the idea that children can do more than we ever imagined when given an appropriate environment to foster those gifts and talents. In that school, the children were learning two foreign languages. They had a sense of community and belonging. Although it was a school, it felt like a family. It was an optimal learning space where creativity and enthusiasm could run wild!

Chapter 18

꧁ᦓꦶꦴꦴꧏ

Pause. Think.

Babies, toddlers, and children are taking in a plethora of information all the time! One of the best ways we can help our children to become independent, creative thinkers it to actually allow them time to think. Read this next sentence and then take a minute to close your else to think about it. Have you ever noticed how many times adults ask children questions and then supply them with an answer before the child has time to respond? This happens quite often! It is important to allow children time to think and not be quick to intervene on their behalf.

When you ask your little one a question, allow them time to process what you have asked and come up with an answer. If the answer is unrelated to what you asked, help them process other ways to receive the question you asked. If the answer is not accurate, be gentle in your correction, if correction is even necessary. Sometimes, you can thank them for their response and guide them with a discussion of a more accurate response.

If you take the time to listen, children actually have really great ideas. We turn to both of our children for help with "complex problems" often. Please do not read this as, "we have our children dealing with adult issues." We may or may not use their ideas. That's the case with adults too though. I may ask your opinion and not use it. However, I now have more information to help me with my problem-solving. When you ask children for their opinion, you empower them. First, children see you as human. Many times, adults present themselves as not capable of making mistakes. Children need to know that you are imperfect too. They need to hear you apologize. They need you to hear their voice as valuable and view their opinion as valid too.

Chapter 19

Build a Spirit of Success

Guess what? Learning is a process in which we make mistakes. I know you knew that already. I'm bringing it up now because it's important to remember this when teaching children. How many times have you been fussed at for trying something and not being successful? It sucks! Children have feelings like we do. They have exponentially more to learn when they are young than we do as adults. Well, maybe that's not true. We are learning different information. Nonetheless, the point is that children are learning and they are learning a lot. One way they learn is by experimentation. Another way they learn is by exploring their curiosity. They also learn by making mistakes.

One thing we can do to help children be successful in their learning process it to be forgiving of their mistakes. If your toddler is learning independence by pouring milk and they spill some, does it benefit them for you to yell at them? Does it benefit you? Not really. In fact, it may be more harmful than anything else. In this instance, here's a trick I learned from a friend. Open an empty dishwasher (read this as not having knives, forks, or things that can harm your little one), let them put the cup down on the open door, and let them pour the milk into the cup over the open dishwasher door. If there is a spill, fill your dishwasher, and run a load of dishes. Problem solved and your little one felt a little bit of success with pouring their own drink and exercising a little independence.

There is one thing that I always wanted to be mindful as we raise our children. We thought hard and were intentional with naming our children. I have always hoped that our children would love their names as much as we do. One way we hope to foster this love is if their name is always, or more often than not, associated with being praised for what they are doing right instead of being connected with what they are doing wrong. If mistakes can be approached in a positive way, which helps children build positive self-esteem and the confidence to attempt new learning challenges. How many of you like to go to work and hear, "Jashaun, this report is awful. What were you thinking? We can't move forward with the project with this kind of work?" Wow! Self-esteem took a major hit. Now Jashaun's report may have sucked. Certainly, approaching it in a different way would have Jashaun in a spirit of learning at this moment instead of dreading making the corrections and risking that feedback again. What if the person who made this comment took a few moments to offer suggestions for improvements in a positive way? Then Jashaun walks away empowered with ways to polish the report to make it ready for the meeting. Even better, what if Jashaun walks into work and hears, "Hey Jashaun! Good morning! Let's talk about that report you submitted. It was awesome and I want to go over a few recommendations with you. I also want to get some tips about how you did the chart discussing the financials." Children are the same way. They want you to love them and they want to feel praised for the hard work they do. Their work may seem basic to us. Remember that each stage of life offers challenges that have never been encountered before. Approach learning with love and encourage children to explore their curiosity, letting them know you support them and are proud of their effort.

Chapter 20

Read

M ore data to blow your mind! As reported by the American Psychological Association, "Children's initial reading competency is correlated with the home literacy environment, the number of books owned, and parent distress (Aikens & Barbarin, 2008; Bergen, Zuijen, Bishop, & Jong, 2016). However, poor households have less access to learning materials and experiences, including books, computers, stimulating toys, skill-building lessons, or tutors to create a positive literacy environment (Bradley, Corwyn, McAdoo, & García Coll, 2001; Orr, 2003)."

How do we change this narrative? I suspect if you are reading this book, access to reading materials may not be your issues. Let's run two thoughts by you though. If you are in a situation where buying a ton of books is not an option, you're in luck! We were not lacking with resources, though we often lacked finances. Let me break it down for you. We may not have money to spend $10-$25 for each book but we do have libraries where we have access to books for the low, low price of free! Be sure to return that book on time though to avoid late fees. How cool is it for your toddler to have their own library card, where they can check out their own books. Nervous about losing the books? Sit there and read the books while you're still in the library! What a great way to spend some time with your little one.

Do you have problems like my family where we love having books in the house but don't always have the financial resources to fund that habit? Library book sales are a book lover's wonderland! Books typically range between $0.25-$1.00. Can't beat that for a purchased book! The best part is that it's much easier to part with a book you didn't pay much for when you are ready to clean your house and pass read books on to other book lovers. Somewhere online, I saw the idea of having a countdown to Christmas with a book each day. We were able to get all new books throughout the year and save them because we used the library book sales to get other books to read throughout the year. We cannot use the lack of resources as our excuse for why our children do not have access to opportunities. Change the narrative. Raise the Bar on Learning!

I hope you're catching on that parenting with intentionality and raising the bar on learning doesn't have to be expensive but it will cost you. It will cost you time and even though that's one of the hardest resources to come across, it's one that we all can access and use to our advantage. There's no magic formula and none of these tips and strategies work every single time and with every single child. However, having some aim and plan about parenting with intentionality is a great place to start.

Chapter 21

❧⳥⳥❧

Spotlight

I know most people reading this book have heard of the game, "20 Questions." One of the best ways to foster an open line of communication with your little one is to begin asking questions about their day at an early age. Let me put on my psychologist hat for just a minute. There are two types of questions, closed-ended questions, and open-ended questions. Closed-ended questions are questions that can be answered with a simple, "yes" or "no." response. For example, "Did you have a good day at school?" The answer could be "yes" or "no" and now your child has moved on. Open-ended questions encourage further explanation like, "Tell me about your day at school." See the difference? We started asking open-ended questions with both of our children as soon as they could talk. Besides modeling how to have a conversation, asking open-ended questions allows you an opportunity to take a glimpse into their day. Children will be children. You may not get all the details you would want to know about. You will be off to a great start though. Another thing that can be discovered through discussing your day via open-ended questions is how they are being treated by others.

I'm going to devote the rest of this chapter to a pool of questions that we choose from to ask our children daily. Yes, we even ask the two-year-old open-ended questions. Also, be mindful not to "lead the witness" with your questions. Children are so quick. If they see you fishing, they may lead you astray or they may dramatically feed it. Be open to hearing their responses. Be available to discuss their responses and their feelings about their communications and activities for the day.

Helping Others -

- Who did you help today?
- How did you help Jason today?
- How do you think Jason felt when you helped him?
- What makes you think he felt that way?
- How did you feel when you helped Jason today?

If you ask the questions above, about helping others, and your little guy cannot think of a way they helped someone today, you can help. The goal is to let your little one know that he is valuable. He is a valuable member of the team. He is a contributing member of the group. He has the power to make a difference in his community. If you ask the questions above and your little one cannot think of how they helped, you can help by asking if he was a good role model or a good leader. Did he help the teacher by listening when the teacher asked the class to sit quietly while she prepared the lesson on the whiteboard? What your daughter a good role model by standing quietly in line when walking in the hallway? These are ways that your children can "help" the teacher. Then you can challenge your daughter to help a peer the next day. If a child drops their pencil, a student with an injured arm needs help carrying their books to the next class, or a friend did not get their assignment while they were in the restroom. These are all ways that even the smallest child can help in the classroom. Eventually, they will be able to independently answer questions about who and how they helped someone else at school each day.

- What did you learn today? (could be random facts, could be academic, or it could be any combination of what was learned at school)

Class and school culture:

- Were you nice to anyone?
- Was anyone nice to you?
- Were you not nice to anyone?
- Was anyone not nice to you?
- Was anyone not nice to anyone else?

Did you catch what I was doing with these questions? Now, we are putting out feelers to detect early signs of bullying and/or abuse, which we, of course, don't want to ever be an issue. I'm checking to see if there are friendships at school. Is your child playing alone or do they have friends? Are they being respected by their peers and adults around them?

- Who taught you that?
- Who said that?
- Where did you learn that?
- Who says that?

Sometimes children come home with new "key phrases" or trendy "words" that are being commonly said at school. That's when I really get into the questions above. I want to know who said it, how they said it when it was said, and who they were talking to and with when it was said. This also helps me get to the bottom of situations if my child can learn to listen and accurately report the details of a situation.

- Tell me something amazing about your day.
- Tell me something you would change about your day.

What we hope will happen here is that we will create a desire for your children to talk to you about anything and everything. When we create a space that is safe for children to talk about things that may not be as important now, they will hopefully know they can talk to you about things that are more important later on in life. It's crucial that we let our children know that their opinion is valuable, we have time and care to hear about their thoughts and feelings now.

Chapter 22

※❦(✿❀)❦※

Logic Wins

Chinenye and I often laugh because his Dad has told his Mom and us many times that we teach our children random skills and then are surprised when they use what we teach them. It's true. Here's a story of when Kemery was maybe two- or three-years-old. At the time, she was in attending school. She loved to wear dresses. I would let her wear the dresses but would put on leggings or pants, even jeans under the dress. I explained to her that she would wear the pants to keep from messing up her knees if she fell down, among other reasons, like being prepared in case a two-year old was climbing on things and not sitting like a young lady in her dress at school. I did not want to inhibit her playing. At the time, one of her best friend's (still is one of her best friend's) was a little girl who always wore big beautiful hair bows and she would sometimes wear frilly lacy socks. One morning, Kemery asked if she could wear her "church" socks to school like her friend. First, we talked about not doing things to be like other people. Had to take that teachable moment though I know she just wanted to wear the socks because she liked them. I told she couldn't wear the socks to school because the school she attended at the time had all of the students to take their shoes off when indoors. I told her the socks were slippery and she could fall. Her rebuttal was that I made her wear pants so that if she fell, she would be less likely to get hurt. Well, the score was Kemery=1, Mommy=0. When you have had a child that small who can think, reason, and logically state their case, sometimes you have to let them win. One might argue that she was talking back. Maybe. At that age, I don't think she had awareness of intentionally talking back and being argumentative. She was pleading her case and she gave a logical explanation as to why I should listen to her. I let her wear the socks to school. I want my children to know that "No" may be the final answer sometimes but it's not always the final answer. There are times when it is acceptable to ask for more. On a job, it's okay to ask for a bigger salary. At school, if you think your grade was unfair, it's okay to ask questions. This is a great skill to have. As our children get older, we do have to be careful to teach them when it is acceptable to use this skill and when it is not acceptable. The goal is to teach them how to think and how to communicate their thoughts and ideas.

Here's another example. Kemery has another friend. Her mom and I were talking about how I believe it is our fault that Kemery does not do much with a spirit of urgency. How did we contribute to this issue? We encouraged taking the time to appreciate life. We would take walks. We stopped to watch ants work. The ants made ant hills or carried food across the sidewalk. We stopped to watch the petals blow off dandelions in the wind. We allowed her the opportunity to explore her surroundings. This is wonderful for a curious toddler. In today's society though, as a child, teen, young adult, or adult sometimes we have to "move it!" Kemery's friend's Mom referred to Kemery's friend as her, "walk through the daffodils child." She, too, took the time to appreciate the world around her. In other words, neither of our babies move expeditiously. Sometimes they are plain old SLOW! Can they move quickly? Of course! The motivation to move is not there. They are both easily stopped by their great ideas, the reorganization of books, or rediscovering an old science kit. Exploring the world around them. One day, I told Kemery we need to move fast like a rabbit! She looked at me and with all sincerity and calmness said, "But Mommy, the tortoise won the race." UGH!!! Dang it! She was right again! Kemery=2, Mommy=0

The thing is that we want them to learn the skills. We want them to be able to be critical thinkers. We want them to be able to communicate their ideas. Yes, there will be many times where this will backfire on you. It's okay. It keeps you on your toes. We have to teach them to apply the skills at appropriate times and to celebrate (sometimes secretly so they won't know they've won every battle) that they are using the skills they have been acquiring. I'll talk more about channeling those skills for good.

Chapter 23

Bossy?
Yes! CEO to be Exact

Kemery and Jeremy have both always been take charge kind of children. They are both very sweet, loving, and thoughtful. They are thinkers. They are intentional and deliberate. They don't back down easily from going after their goals. Some call this being bossy. In an effort to channel positive energy over our children, we have chosen to refer to those "bossy" qualities as CEO qualities. Truth be told, top executives exhibit similar qualities. They think outside of the box. They don't take everything for face value. They know how to tactfully challenge authority. CEOs also know how to delegate and work well with others. All of these are top notch qualities when used correctly and at appropriate times. An eight-year-old who uses her CEO qualities to avoid going to bed after being told to go to bed may get into trouble with the top executives in the household. However, we do not want to silence that voice inside of them that tells them to stand up for what they believe, when it is appropriate to do so.

Here's an example. For those of you who know me personally, I bet you were wondering where I would talk about this. I'm not going to go into a ton of detail here. I certainly think it's worth mentioning though. In telling children to let their lights shine brightly, I must share this example. Kemery is fluent in Japanese. She has been learning since she was 13-months old. She and her classmates were invited by their teacher to visit Japan. Sadly, we had to tell her we could not go because we did not have the discretionary funds to make the trip. Kemery's a wonderful girl and her logic can surpass all adult understanding at times. She has an amazing ability to be understanding, reasonable, and patient. She said, "okay" though Chinenye and I knew the news was disappointing. A few days passed and it was Martin Luther King, Jr. Day in 2017, when she came to me and said, "Mommy, I want to work from home today." I asked for more information. She said, "I want to work on my business plan, my business cards, and my logo. I want to earn the money to go to Japan." She was eight-years old.

I sat there and took in that moment. I could tell by the look in her eyes that she was serious. I also knew that whatever I said could shape her thoughts on how we perceived her ability to achieve her goal and manifest her dream into reality. Even if we disagreed and ultimately decided against moving forward, this had to be handled with care. We sat down and talked about it. We listened to her reasoning and her plan. Chinenye and I discussed with her and without her. We knew that with the trip being a short time away, we would have to be all in or tell her she could not start a business. I'm certain you have a good idea of what we decided. We said, "Let's rock!" In a short amount of time, Kemery had raised and earned (a combination of business profit and donations) about $5000. Unfortunately, we needed about $9000 to $12000 to go on the trip. Close but not close enough. Disappointed again but not discouraged. Kemery started that business in February 2018 and almost two years later, she is still laser focused toward the goal. She is also laser focused on helping others, which makes my heart full.

In this past year alone, Kemery started the year with her leather bracelets, that she custom engraves in Japanese, being included in the swag bags of the 2018 Teen Choice Awards. Kemery's clothing line had 18 outfits featured on the runway of Atlantic City Fashion Week in February. Our City Council Woman reached out to me to invite us to the next meeting where they declared June 24, 2018 Kemery Kreates' Appreciation Day for all of the cool stuff she'd been doing with her business and in the community. She became a published author when she wrote a chapter in a collaborative book with 25 other young moguls who came together to share their secrets to success and encourage other children to go after the dreams. She and I were included in the 18th Anniversary Edition of Who's Who in Black Atlanta. Kemery was awarded a grant and was able to start teaching Japanese courses online and she able to run her first entrepreneurship program that she has been teaching to the teens at the local YMCA. Together, they spent over 100 hours going over the basics of owning a business and they ended by launching their own business. At their first expo, they earned over $200 in three hours, with a profit of almost $100! This year, she also had several media opportunities and was included in some magazines, including Teen Boss and Black Hustle Magazine.

All of that happened within this past year. I couldn't make this stuff up if I tried! What if we had told her, "No?" It would not have been the end of the world. She would have bounced back and been okay. I honestly believe that is all true. However, we chose to say, "Yes," this time and I think that even if she decides to move on tomorrow, she has accomplished feats that many adults won't accomplish in their entire lifetime. I want her to remember that we believed in her and that because she believed in herself, had the courage to take action, and had the heart to serve, she has been an agent of change in the lives of others at the tender age of 10-years-old. She has not been to Japan yet and I look forward to capturing the moments when she holds the plane ticket in her hand, get the stamp on her passport, and when her feet land on solid ground.

As for baby brother, his day care teacher set up a lemonade stand. They practiced all week. All of the children helped make the lemonade. We received a message to come with cash and coins in hand to support the tiny entrepreneurs because they were saving their money for a bubble blower.

Of course, all parents obliged. When I went to pick up our little guy, there he stood waiting for his turn to sell Mommy some lemonade. He's been to many vending events with the family as we support his big sister in her entrepreneurship goals. I walked up to the lemonade stand and asked for one cup of lemonade. Beaming with excitement, he, with his two-year-old self, picked up the lemonade pitcher with both hands. His elbows were high as he worked hard to control the pitcher full of lemonade. He poured my lemonade and told me it cost one dollar. He reached out his tiny hand for his money. I gave him the money in coins. I watched him put each coin in their toy cash register. He handed me a napkin and then my cup of lemonade. I took a sip and it was actually quite yummy. Next thing I know, Jeremy came from around the stand to get some lemonade from my cup! Well, it was good while it lasted! I love that we can start early instilling the confidence children need to know they, too, can accomplish great things. We believe in their ability to positively impact the world, in a way that works for them, in a way that brings them joy.

Chapter 24

❧⟨✿⟩❧

It's Not Always About You

For Chinenye and I, it has always been important that we remember that life is not always about us. When we are part of a larger community, it's important that we serve our community. That community could be our family, our friends, or the people around us. One of the activities that we enjoy doing as a family, is running or even going for walks. Although we did not know each other when we were growing up, it's wonderfully coincidental that Chinenye's parents and my parents instilled in us and our brothers and sisters, the importance of helping other people. I have been volunteering in my community since I was in elementary school, and Chinenye the same. As such, he and I are in full agreeance that our children should value the importance of giving back.

How do you teach volunteerism to a young child? My Mom and I used to walk in the breast cancer walk for research when I was in high school and college. When Kemery turned three-years-old, I learned that there is a family walk of one mile for the same breast cancer walk. We signed up and walked as a family. We made a big deal of it for Kemery. Since she was so small, we actually trained. We drove around our neighborhood to find the half-mile mark. Then we would walk a little further each time until we were able to make it to the half-mile mark and back with no problem. We stretched in the yard before and after the race. On race day, Kemery was so excited. Toward the end of the race, she began to get tired. We stopped to rest and told her how much further she had left. She could make the decision to finish what she started or we would pick her up and carry her to the end. We were totally okay with whatever answer she decided. After all, she was only three-years-old. She decided she wanted to finish the race. The end was so close. We were totally cheering her on. We walked that race every year until I was pregnant with her brother (five-years later). At some point, we switched from the one-mile walk to the three-mile walk. Kemery has now completed 21 races, in three states, and four of the races were triathlons. Some of those races were to raise money for causes. Other races were for fun.

I loved the idea of small children giving back so much that I incorporated similar opportunities through my business, Raise the Bar Learning, LLC. We did virtual races to raise money for breast cancer research. Kemery would walk with us and little friends, mostly on the East Coast, would walk wherever they were. We had medals made and shirts. They would take pictures and send them in. The idea is that the children can see that they can make a difference when they work together. One year we sent stickers to the village where Chinenye's family is from in Nigeria. Another year, we collected and sent school supplies to the same village. There was a project where children wrote letters and drew pictures for a little girl who was battling cancer.

Now, Kemery enjoys giving back in different ways like volunteering with the youth ministry at church, sorting vegetables at a local vegetable co-op, and most recently, teaching her entrepreneurship program at the local YMCA. Maybe I should revisit that program for children volunteering. Jeremy is two-years-old and has a heart for sharing...usually. Stay connected with us if this is an interest you'd like to pursue with your little ones. All of our projects have been able to be completed at home or where you live. I am open to the idea of a local project where many children could meet and volunteer together.

Chapter 25

Power Parenting with Penny Pockets

W hen you look at all of the activities and events that our children attend and participate in, we have found that some people have made judgments about how much we must spend on these opportunities. In full transparency, we are grateful for what we have though our cup has not exactly runneth over in the area of financial abundance. As I was taught from a friend when I was in college, we live on the humble. However, we are rich in so many other ways. Our children do not lack in opportunities because with the access to technology, information, and resources right at our fingertips, there is no reason for us to lack. We have to be creative. Here are some ways we were savvy enough to score some major educational wins.

Activities at Home - Your home is full of opportunities to learn. For example, when you are in the kitchen, cook together. As always, supervision is key. Give your child something they can do and monitor them while they do it. For example, if they can stir the mix, read the directions, or pour the ingredients, let them do that. There is so much that can be learned while cooking together. You can talk about fractions (pizza), sorting (beans or vegetables versus fruit), colors (matching food items), measurement (pouring ingredients), or reading (going through a recipe together).

One activity we did with Kemery when she was younger was to pour water into clear empty bottles. We added food coloring to each bottle. Supervised closely, we let her help with this process. We let her help with mixing some colors like red and blue to make purple. Sounds like basic chemistry with toddlers. This is where it starts. Then, we taped the tops of the bottles closed. She was a toddler and she played with the bottles for at least a week, supervised, of course. She could roll the bottles. She could shake the bottles. We counted the bottles. We named the colors. She could pick out the colors if we named them or we could line them up and let her name the colors. There is so much that can be done with things you already one. Education does not have to cost money as much as it costs time. Raise the Bar on Learning!

Word Games - I know we had an entire section on increasing vocabulary. I am leaving this here because I want you to see these games as an activity for learning that does not cost money. Kemery was very young when she learned about personification. We were at the eye doctor's office, sitting in the waiting room. There was a picture on the wall. The sun had a happy face. We took that opportunity to point out the sun. We asked questions like "When we go outside, does the sun really have a happy face?" Then we talked about other books where inanimate objects had faces like people, like "Thomas the Train." After each example was given, we said, "That's personification." It was as easy as that. From that point on, she knew personification. We did the same with alliteration. She's known that term since she was a toddler.

Reuse Toys for Different Purposes - Do you know the blocks they make now? I'm talking about the blocks that are made of that baby safe rubber or plastic. These blocks come sold in a set with numbers or in a set with letters. The blocks also have animals on the sides. The animal names start with the letter on the block. These blocks serve multiple purposes and the purpose changes with age and developmental progress. For example, when our daughter was birth-6 months, she was grasping the blocks, first with two hands and then with one hand. The blocks are not hard so she experimented with taste (after we washed them, of course). We would build little towers and she would crawl over and knock the blocks down. Then, when she was 17 months old, she advanced to stacking the blocks, naming the colors, identifying the animals, identifying the letters, and identifying the letters. Once she mastered identifying the colors, we moved on to sorting by colors. By practicing all of the skills mentioned, skills are developed in the areas of creativity, cognitive (thinking) ability, fine motor skills, visual-motor integration, and basic academics. Remember, learning should be fun. No need to stress your little one to catch on. Introduce the concept and practice the concepts during play. Your baby will catch on in their own time. We love toys with multiple functions!

Vacation - There was a time where I was working at a company that had amazing benefits. The salary was not bad but with a two-hour commute (each way) and $400/month spent on gas, after doing the math, it was not in our benefit. However, we completely take advantage of the opportunity to use the benefits we had access to at the time. The company offered a wellness program. Every month we could log in the amount of time we spent exercising and maintaining our health goals to receive points. We received points for going to the doctor for preventative check-ups and wellness checks. We also received points for major fitness events like running a 5k or 10k. I committed to the goals, logged them in and received points. I saved my points for the year and cashed out with gift cards to benefit different vacations.

Here's what I did. I was fortunate enough that while I worked for this company, one of the professional organization I am a member of happened to have two conferences in Florida. The company reimbursed for the conference as it was related to my job description and was professional learning. Since Chinenye is a teacher, he pitched the conference to his principal and since it was a school psychology conference, his pitch was accepted. We both now have approved leave. Are you following me? My company would pay for travel. I could get some amazing price on a flight and take myself to the conference in luxury or I could drive to the conference and use that money to pay for gas. Driving allowed me to take the entire family. We are all now in Florida, right? Great! My company would also pay for a hotel, right? After doing a little research, I found an amazing home to rent that cost less than the conference hotel. The house was a 3-bedroom home with a kitchen, garage, and a swimming pool. Still winning! Please note that throughout this process, I always make sure that my company is winning too! No red flags. We do not try to cheat our company out of anything. We are making the best use of our resources while making sure that everyone comes out on top! We now have a place to stay and a way to get there. My company paid a per diem for food each day. We could go out to eat but only my food would be covered. Instead of going out to eat, we went to the grocery store. We made pans of lasagna before leaving home to keep us from having to cook a lot while on vacation. We stuck the food in a cooler and drove it to the vacation home. When we arrived, we bought staples like drinks, salad, and fruits. All of that cost less than me going out to eat so my company is still winning. Remember all of the points that were saved throughout of the year for me taking care of myself and taking the time to log them in? One of the gift cards I could redeem the points for was a Disney gift card! Winning!! I redeemed all of my points for hundreds of dollars in Disney gift cards! We had enough for our daughter to get the Disney princess makeover and for us to have dinner with the princesses!

The icing on the cake? At the time, we were a family of three. What did we do with the three-bedroom home, when we only needed two bedrooms? We invited grandparents to come! They had a room, we had a room, and Kemery had a room! We got a great deal on the house. We arrived a few days early and because we got such a great deal on the house, the entire stay was still less than the few days of the conference we stayed at the conference hotel. In those few extra days, we drove an hour or two further and spent some time at the beach. On conference days, Kemery stayed with her grandparents while Chinenye and I went to the conference. Then, we picked up Kemery and headed to the theme parks. After doing research, we had amazing prices for park tickets too! Seriously, the fun we had on this trip would have cost a fortune but using our resources and doing research made this trip next to nothing for us.

Summer Camp - Stay connected. One of the benefits of connecting with Raise the Bar Learning, LLC is to help parents find resources, along the way, to help each other offer our children the best opportunities for success - in raising whole, healthy children. This tip comes from being connected with other parents who are on the same journey. Kemery attended a three-week long Engineering Camp for two consecutive summers. The camp was sponsored by one of the most well-known engineering organizations in the country. The first year, the camp was FREE! The second year, the camp only cost us $50 for the entire three weeks! I cannot make this up. A friend signed up her children and called me to tell me about it. Given Chinenye's degree is in Industrial Engineering, he was totally on board. The sacrifice? We drove 45 minutes each way for her to get there. I don't care about that! What she learned was invaluable! The second year, three of her friends who live closer to us participated and we all carpooled. Win! Win! Win! Kemery loved the first year so much, specifically the chemical engineering. The program sponsors were often the judges of the weekly competitions. I did a little research on the sponsoring Chemical Engineering company and found out they were not far from Grandmommy and Grandaddy's house (about a 4-hour drive). At the end of one of the competitions, I walked up to the representative and told them of our daughter's interest and asked if we could arrange a visit to their plant in New Jersey when we are at Grandmommy and Grandaddy's house for the holidays. We stayed in touch and we received the okay to make a visit. They even let us bring someone. We drove up to visit a cousin that is close to Kemery's age to let him be part of the experience too. The visit was amazing! They were able to see where hundreds of top brands of products get their fragrance! The tour included showing them the process of where and how the chemicals are mixed to make the perfect match. Kemery and her cousin even went home with goody bags! Cost = $0. Well, the cost of gas from Grandmommy and Grandaddy's house to the company which is close to Princeton University and back home. That's it!

Season Passes - We also decided we wanted to get one season pass to a different experience each year. While this is not always in the budget, we sacrificed to make it happen because ultimately, it was less expensive than paying entrance fees for each visit and more valuable than the alternative, which was not going at all. What we learned from having season passes is that the venue was usually more enjoyable. When you pay a lot of money to go to a venue and you only have one opportunity to see everything, you almost feel obligated to stay all day and get to all of the exhibits or all of the activities. That's tough on a toddler or young child. When you have a season pass, stopping in for an hour to see some of the attractions is much more reasonable and can happen when you are "in the neighborhood." It's more enjoyable and it's a perfect rainy day option unless you picked the zoo for your pass. We also like passes that can be used in many locations, preferably nationwide. For example, the Children's Museum has a pass that can be used at locations throughout the nation. This is perfect for a family that takes road trips often. You can visit the museum in multiple cities, in different states, on the same trip, at no additional cost! Sounds like another win to me!

Running Errands - Here's a tip. Running errands can be a chore to you but it's an experience for your child. Shameless plug: Grab a copy of the book Chinenye and I wrote, The Things I See: Scavenger Hunt. You can turn a trip to the grocery store, the bank, the airport, or even the doctor's office into an adventure! The book is an activity book that gives your child things to look for while out running your normal errands. It helps to increase vocabulary because we included a section in the back of the book with definitions of the items, in the way we might explain them to a young child. The fun of using an activity book like this is that you may engage with your child in a totally different way when you are doing things you typically do. How many times have we seen a toddler or young child in the basket with a phone in their hands, playing a game or watching a video while Mom or Dad shops? How many times has this been us? No blame placed here. We've done it too. We do aim to make this the exception and not the rule though. Our goal is to find more opportunities for us to take advantage of teachable moments and decrease the amount of time we spend disconnected from our children.

When we consider the opportunities that can be learned from a simple trip to the grocery store, we then see it as a valuable learning opportunity. The cool part is that the grocery store has numerous learning opportunities. We can talk about the colors of fruits and vegetables. Then, we can sort fruits and vegetables. One of the things we started with Kemery at an early age is reading labels. It started out at a very basic level. Low sugar, high protein, high dietary fiber, low cholesterol are all good, for example. Then reading the ingredients was another skill. Kemery learned to read when she 2.5 years old. Her vocabulary increased exponentially after she learned how to read. When we read labels, we looked for keywords, for example, words ending in -ose usually meant a form of sugar. We looked to see the order of the ingredients and learned that the ingredients with the most contents included were usually listed first. As she got older, we could talk about percentages. We looked at the cost per ounce on different items and compared the prices of the products. Here's another big one...budgeting and estimation. At the grocery store, we can go in with a budget and as we select items and add them to our cart, we can add the cost to our total and make a close estimate of how much we are spending to make sure we do not exceed our budget. Yes, this is important for those among us where a trip to the grocery store could happen without requiring a specific budget. These are skills all children, future adults, would benefit from knowing. While I'm not an extreme couponer, I don't like to leave money on the table. We do talk about using coupons when I remember to do it.

Investing - Now that we are saving all of this money or not spending all of the money, depending on your perspective, it is important for children to know the value of investing, not just saving. I'm certainly no expert on investing though we do have an account for each of our children that we use to put in whatever we can, whenever we can. We do not place value on having name brand items as much as we place value on owning stock in companies. Using what we know, we explain what we can about when to buy and when to sell stocks. We show Kemery her portfolio and let her see how the stocks are doing. Stocks can be very inexpensive so if you can afford one stock each paycheck, find one and invest in it. Remember to do some research and to use money that won't hurt you if you lose it. There are even programs now that will let you buy a piece of a more expensive stock. It's easier than ever to try your hand at investing. The more educated you are though, the more your return on investment, which is the ultimate goal. The information is available. Plug into a resource that works for you and let your children be part of this learning process.

Chapter 26

No Limits.
No Boundaries.

Our paths to acquiring knowledge may be different and that's okay as long as we don't prematurely put a cap on our possibilities. No limits. No boundaries. I'm a big advocate of not putting limitations on what children can do yet I still fall short of being consistent with that sometimes.

One day, Kemery was playing with her little brother, Jeremy, and tried to get him to sit criss-cross applesauce. He was still very small, barely sitting up by himself. I let her know that he could not do that yet because his legs were too short and he was not big enough yet. A few days later, I looked down and he was sitting criss-cross applesauce! I thought to myself, "Come on, Mommy, no limits, no boundaries!" I had to let Kemery know she was right and that grown-ups do not always hit the nail on the head. Tell your children to dream big and don't ever let someone tell them that they cannot do something they believe they can do. Don't accept other people's limitations of them.

My husband and I published a book a few years ago. The book was published and we later found a typo in the published book. One typo? It's okay, right? For us, we were upset because we had both reviewed the manuscript multiple times. We then paid an editor and proofreader to go through the manuscript. It went to print and there was the typo! How could we all have missed that? I published another book that same year. Chinenye and I both read and reread the manuscript before sending it to the editor and proofreader. Kemery was about six-years-old when I was writing that book. She asked if she could read it. It was a children's book.

Of course I let Kemery read my book. What better way to find if children would like the book than to let our own child read it? You wouldn't believe that she found an error! I used the wrong homophone and she found that error! Chinenye and I both missed it, as well as the editor we hired. Kemery caught the mistake before going to print! We made the correction and the book went to print. I Chinenye and I are also working on another book that we hope to release soon after this one. We hired an editor and I caught multiple mistakes. Keep reading to see our solution. Since adding her input on my last children's book, Kemery has edited another children's book, though the author has not gone to print with that book yet. She also helped edit parts of the collaborative book that she co-authored earlier this year. As such, I am confident that her track record yields great results. That being said, go back and check the front of this book to see who we trusted with editing this book and who we will trust with editing our next book. As you read this book and the next, I hope that you don't read with a critical eye. Instead, I hope you read with the appreciation for us being able to empower our daughter to know that we trust her gifts and talents enough to hire her to edit works that we are actually publishing. I hope that whatever your child discovers as their gifts, talents, and passion, that you will help them to believe that they're ability to make a difference is real.

Chapter 27

※✧(ʕ◔ϖ◔ʔ)✧※

Make Learning Fun

ave you ever been doing something fun when somebody interrupts your fun by wanting you to do something way less fun? Think about life from a child's perspective. How many times has your child been playing with their toys and you stop them to eat dinner? How many times have you been out at the park and when it was time to go, you were met with resistance because being at the park is way more fun than being trapped in a car seat only to head home and take a bath. In these scenarios, we probably agree that there is time for play and time to accomplish other tasks.

My challenge is that we take a look at how we can make the learning experience fun, so much fun that children never want to stop learning. Once we have consistently implemented strategies to make learning fun, there seems to be some intrinsic motivation that occurs. Children are sparked by their own curiosity and develop their own desire to want to learn more. When learning is a series of games and an activity they deem as fun, the difficulty will be in figuring out how to find more time for them to learn! Honestly, this is one of the challenges we currently face with Kemery. She loves learning for the sake of learning. This contributes to to her deficit in being able to move expeditiously. She stops to read everything. She wants to do experiments. She wants to research new ideas and past history. Baby brother, Jeremy, though only two-years-old, also has the same thirst for knowledge. He enjoys doing "flashcards." I'll drop some insight on flashcards in a moment.

How many of you have ever found flashcards to be an effective tool to learn new information? I'm raising my hand. I used this strategy often throughout my school experience. They help with information that needs to be memorized, like sight words, for example. It wasn't until I was an adult that I learned the way I had been studying with flashcards was the "old way." You know how we used to study with flashcards. If you get it right you get to keep it and if you miss the word or definition, it went back in the pile in hopes that you get it correct next time. Check this out. The research I read at some point in my school psychology days, is that a more effective strategy is to go through the flashcards separating the items you get correct from the items you need to review again. Before starting over, mix in some of the words that were correct? Why do that when you already know the information? It builds in opportunities for success. Everyone wants to celebrate for getting one right. When you set yourself up for repeated perceived failure, that can become discouraging. That was a fun fact for older children (elementary school) through adults. Now, let's get back to our babies.

As you can imagine, flashcards for our two-year-old are different. He has a variety of flashcards. His favorite cards are the touch and feel cards. They have shapes, colors, animals, transportation, and food. They all have something he can feel, some texture experience (bumpy, sticky, soft, furry, etc). Now, we are working on words and he actually enjoys the homemade flashcards with letters and word families. We put them together to make different word families. He loves them. We apply the same concept as above though. When we introduce new words, we also introduce words that he can read with accuracy almost every time. He gets over-the-moon excited when he gets it right because we praise, praise, praise him! We cheer! High-fives and fist bumps are huge! We celebrate the victory! It is more important for us to let him the own the victory than it is for us to dwell on what he did not right. Why? He's only two-years-old. We are simply exposing him to the information. If he gets it right, great! If he does not get it immediately, it's okay. There's time.

Back to making learning fun. Here are some ideas to help reframe how we approach learning.

Consider this scenario. We have a child learning fractions. Which option is more fun, completing a worksheet or making a pizza with a tortilla shell, some sauce, and cheese and using a pizza cutter to determine the fraction of the pizza that each person in the house will eat?

Consider this scenario. We have a child practicing phonics. Which option is more fun, a reading passage or reading an easy recipe to help your family make a meal or some cookies?

Consider this scenario. We have a child learning how to write. Which option is more fun, copying letters and sentences with a paper and pencil or writing in shaving cream on the kitchen table or counter? If you choose the latter, which I hope you do because it is quite fun, please be certain to monitor closely. Even if your little one is advanced and can handle the practice of writing, we must stay vigilant and be reminded that they are still developing like a two-year-old and may be tempted to have those hands head for the mouth.

Although I often buy our children toys or teaching resources that are "technically" geared for children above their chronological age (I may get a toy that is for a three-year-old for our two-year-old, not a toy that is for 10-year-olds for a two-year-old), they are NEVER unattended while using these items. Safety is the first order of business. If you choose to do the same, please always consider the potential dangers, stay actively engaged and aware during the learning experience, be proactive with safety, and remove the items once the activity is completed.

Naturally, when something is fun and exciting, we never want to stop doing it. Keep this in mind as you navigate the nuances and joys of educating your little one. When learning is fun, they will never want to stop learning.

As I share with you all of these great techniques to Raise the Bar on Learning, I encourage you to keep in mind that babies, toddlers, and children may be more advanced cognitively but that does not always, or even usually, translate to emotional and behavioral age. Although we can give our little ones the skills to communicate, which significantly decreases frustration, it is important to understand that young children are still developing in other ways. They still need to run and play. They need to use their imagination. They need free time to safely explore the world around them. Children need to cry, laugh, and express a range of emotions. When exposing children to different skills, keep in mind that learning should be fun and not stressful. Children will make mistakes. You may introduce a concept three, four, or twenty-four times before they begin to pick up the skill and that is okay. Also, what works for one may not necessarily work for another. Please avoid the temptation to compare children. They all have their strengths and areas to build on and again, that is a good thing. It's what makes us all unique and wonderful!

After making it to this point in the book, I hope you see the value in nurturing your children. The art of unlocking your child's potential is not solely an academic endeavor. Children have to be in an emotional place where they can receive new information. We have touched on communication (verbal and nonverbal), academics, building confidence, managing tough feelings, empowerment and much more. Children need all of these areas working together, or at least not against each other, if we are hoping to tap into their highest potential. All components working together, combined with creative strategies and the mindset of endless possibilities increases our chances of unlocking our baby's potential!

References

Bradley, R. H., Corwyn, R. F., McAdoo, H. P., & García
  Coll, C. (2001). The home environments of
  children in the United States Part I: Variations by
  age, ethnicity, and poverty status. *Child
  Development, 72,* 1844-1867. doi:10.1111/1467-
  8624.t01-1-00382

GEEARS (2018). First 2000 Days Initiative. Retrieved
  from www.geears.org

5 Books, 3 Authors, 1 Family

The Things I See: Scavenger Hunt
ISBN: 978-1-941592-01-4
Co-authors:
Chinenye O. Oparah and Kia M. Haselrig-Oparah
Published By: Raise the Bar Learning, L.L.C.
www.raisethebarlearning.com

Yum Yum! New Tastes are Fun!
ISBN: 978-1-941592-00-7
Author: Kia M. Haselrig-Oparah
Published By: Raise the Learning, L.L.C.
www.raisethebarlearning.com

The Science Behind It:
Formulating Success At Any Age
ISBN: 978-0-578209-00-5
Author (Book Collaboration): Kemery C. Oparah
www.kemeryoparah.com

25 Exercises to Strengthen Your Parenting Muscles
ISBN: 978-1-941592-04-5
Co-authors:
Chinenye O. Oparah and Kia M. Haselrig-Oparah
Published By: Raise the Bar Learning, L.L.C.
www.raisethebarlearning.com